Tough and Tender:
The Crybaby Collective Volume One

Tough and Tender:
The Crybaby Collective Volume One

The Crybaby Author & Artist Collective

the crybaby club

2017

Cover Art and Chapter Headers illustrated by Natalie Meagan

Copyright © 2017 by **The Crybaby Club**

All rights reserved. This book or any portion thereof may not be reproduced or used in any manner whatsoever without the express written permission of the publisher except for the use of brief quotations in a book review or scholarly journal.

First Printing: 2017

ISBN: 978-0-9986395-0-5

The Crybaby Club: Author & Artist Collective
PO Box 40147
Memphis, TN 38174

www.thecrybabyclub.com

Introduction

If you're reading this, chances are that you know a Crybaby. By a Crybaby, I mean a member of the Crybaby Club – formerly known as the Crybaby Girl Gang, but expanded to be all-inclusive in terms of gender, sexuality, and the likes. The Crybaby Club was founded by some incredible women, worth mentioning now; as we lack a dedication page, I'd like to take a moment to thank **Natalie Meagan**, **Kaitlyn Luckow**, **Kayley Mills**, **Samantha Kirk**, and **Sarah Christiaansen** for making this book and our participation in the club a possibility – and quite frankly, a grand privilege. In the following pages, you will find some works by wonderful human beings who poured their hearts out onto the page – be it poetry, prose, painting, or digital art.

The Crybaby Club is difficult to describe, so we will take the words of a dear Crybaby, Nora Ramaha: "The Crybaby Club is this sort of home feeling. I think I've said this before once, but it still rings true: that you could be having the worst possible day, and the moment you get home, there's someone there waiting for you with arms wide open, ready to listen and bake you cookies and give you hugs. The Crybaby Club is that home. It's that sense of peace when you enter and that sense of comfort of that person that's waiting to hear about your day. That sense of relaxation like a hot cup of tea before bed."

The Crybaby Club can be found online at TheCrybabyClub.com, as well as on Instagram @TheCrybabyClubOfficial, and on Facebook at The Crybaby Club page.

Topics in this book range from Food, to Anxiety, to Self-Care; but with topics as sensitive as Mental Health, I feel inclined to advise any readers that there may be some content that can be inappropriate to young readers or can be considered 'triggering' to those who have had experiences similar to that of the writer. We've chosen to keep these pieces in the book as it is important to acknowledge and accept, not hide, the results of mental traumas. As with your body, it is important to take care of yourself if you are feeling unwell in your mind – so please do not hesitate to seek help if you need it.

So Much Love,
Rhea Smith

Contents

Introduction 2
Chapter 1: Food 7
   An Ode to My Burrito Bowl 8
   Pudding 10
   Orthorexia Nervosa 12
   The Struggle 14
   Tokens 15
   Eat 17
Chapter 2: Fulfillment 18
   The Bitterest Goodbye 19
   My Selfish Muse 22
   Mantra 23
   Blank page. 25
   Disrupting the Image of Beauty 29
Chapter 3: Anxiety 34
   Monsters 35
   Numbers 38
   But Did I? 39
   The Morning After 41
   The Duality of Anxiety 43
   The Fight 45
   Acai Violetta 48
   Anxiety Attack 50
Chapter 4: Self-Care 52
   To My Younger Me 54
   Wash Our Hands I 57
   self-love 59
   Wash Our Hands II 61
   To Care For Me 63
Chapter 5: Mental Health 66
   Losing My Mind 67
   Stigma 70
   Train Tracks 71

There is a Monster in All of Us 74
Medicated 76
The Fight 78

Chapter 6: Love 84
He Is Music 85
Unicorn's Pain and The Heart 86
Stale Breadcrumbs 91
Gunpowder Hearts I 92
Puppy Love 93
Gunpowder Hearts II 94
"You're In Love With A Memory" 95
She Said 96

Chapter 7: Lust 98
She's In Each Of Us 99
Connect 100
Lonely Lust 101
"Boys Like You" 102
Thoughts During Sex 103

Chapter 8: Miscellaneous 104
Talk is Talk is Talk is Talk 105
The Dog and the Butterfly 107
Midnight Blooms I 110
Counting 112
Hole 114
Midnight Blooms II 117
Second Thoughts 119
The Irony That Day 121

About the Collective 122

CHAPTER ONE
food

An Ode to My Burrito Bowl
by Cassandra Bankson

A fragrant mosaic,
Its disproportionate tiles,
Irresistible to eyes hungry for culture and art.
Smooth oblong granules
Attempt to shore up an avalanche of onyx stones,
The way you would find a harbor's old wooden slats and rebar
arguing with the quipping Mediterranean coastline.
Chevrolet Red, shellacked pieces of moist brick
Are marbled with rich, jealous streaks of fluorescent green,
A hue that mirrors the way Pyrénées trails glow in razor cuts of
spring's sunlight.
And if dreams were made of dirt, the resonant Moreno soil gives a
recipe for oversleep.
When you close your eyes and fold your thoughts like napkins
And allow steam to pour into your lungs,
You may have to pull apart your memories like layers of an onion.
The scent of imported history
Thrown into a bed of smooth glass
May scorch your nostrils like the powdered spices that hang in the air
of Spanish markets
If you allow the scrambled tile pieces
To dance the flamenco across your lips
You may smother the hunger that only travel could extinguish.
A brimming bowl of mosaicked culinary art,
The exotic taste of a barcelonian lisp.

Alyssa Paxson

Pudding
by Caz Brett

1.

I see her lying there, beckoning with one finger
a dark lock of her dark hair carelessly caressing her temple.

I know what she wants. I can see. She is hungry, but so am I.

She is belly-up, round folds of skin with dark creases
melting into the armchair.
Her jumper hoisted up by its rough fabric, but not tweed
Inexpensive. Patchy in places.
but not her smooth velvety skin. Soft, and gently rolling.
She is exposed and alone and I want to look away yet I am
addicted to the plush shirring of her body
I want to tell her, yet her warm creamy thigh is flashing like a
beacon and I can't tear my eyes away from the freckle that winks
as she flexes her leg.
Her eyes, oh her eyes. They melt me inside
their wicked flames burn something within me; a soft and
delicate centre that oozes my perversion and drips with saliva
and wit. I charm her.

Her eyes are locked onto me and finally
yes, just like that
but more, I need more
she gently leans forwards, and I eagerly lean up towards her to
glimpse the gaping neckline as it drops towards me and

2.

Once again the unstopping mechanism we call time whiles away my day
and we arrive home exhausted, tumbled through the vacuum packed train that aches and groans across the city.
The smog rolls off me as I roll off my uniform and discard it uncaringly on the floor, where it will lie forlorn until Thursday.
The pause as I unthinkingly do it again. We. That word. That loaded, cruel word.
We were two letters, joined together, only making sense as a couple, a duo. Like us, just two letters, but so warm and tender with intimacy.
I am the single lonely letter, always detached and always flying solo.
My heart reaches out to you with every afflicted limb but I'm torn apart and there is no limb left.
I'm just an echo where there used to be a person and a voice, but now there is just a shadowy reminder that I existed.
Stop it.
I feel it, I burn with desire but I self-douse with a shower of guilt and fading memories of we, of us
of once two letters, now one.
I am starved of you but learning what it means to be without you.
Stop it.
Casting my eyes about the room, my amatory senses awaken. I prepared for this. I fucking prepared.
A conquest to be had, an affair to be met and forgotten: my aphrodisiac knight in shining armour, my sick fantasy.
I lick my lips and sink into the forgiving armchair and I forget to judge myself, but I'm judging the sweet divine pudding of my dreams staring back at me.
No longer I, but back to me. Now us, now we. I already have a fork in my hand, and there is no time for flirting. I'm an uncouth, capricious delinquent with no time for manners, I lean forwards, and I cry like a baby as I devour you whole.

Orthorexia Nervosa
by Meg Colt

Kale, quinoa, chia seeds, come and GET them!
These superfoods are your ticket to health, wealth,
and ACCEPTANCE.

Obsession, fear of sugar, jump on and EXPERIENCE it!
Forget that donut silly, your body is a TEMPLE,
don't you dare LITTER it with that.

I'm not a demon, I'm your own personal COACH.
Look at how well I'm taking CARE of you,
making sure those numbers keep getting SMALLER.
The smaller you are, the GREATER your existence.
This is about your SPIRIT!
LARGE spirit, SMALL body, that's the goal darling.

Why aren't those numbers getting SMALLER anymore?
Well, that's YOUR fault,
you must not be doing something right.
Let's CUT more food groups.
How about ALL added sugar, you can't be having that.
Forget lunch dates with friends, you don't NEED those.
You are going to be the picture of HEALTH,
who needs friends anyway?

WHY are you crying?
I'm HELPING you dear, keep going!
You CAN do this, you can do anything.
Well, as long as you have ME anyway.
This is all the rage, what's in FASHION.

There isn't anything WRONG,
WHY are you doubting me?
There are SO many other people doing this,
it's perfectly FINE.

STOP questioning me, I mean it.
DON'T listen to those body positive people,
they are just FOOLS who don't care about their health.

You can't get rid of me, I'm NOT done with you!
Don't do this, don't PUSH me away!

You may have succeeded for now,
but just you WAIT dear girl.

I'll be here waiting.

The Struggle
by Rebecca Foley

where did it go
one moment it's there
one taste
next thing I know
it's gone
food on my plate
where did it go

Tokens
by Haley Littlefield

It is a cold morning, not unlike any other
Yet, tiny rainbows float in a stark white pool

Among images of luck and greed, lust and love
Shiny gold stars and pale crescent moons,
A lavender token signaling one creature's domestication,
A faded crimson symbol of another's inflated ego
Surrounded by a lemon-colored reminder of time's cruel passage

All these lay against a plain, yet mysterious background
Flat, beige colored shapes, perhaps a bell and a fish
Crosses and triangles, possibly images of a time long gone
Shapes that have lost their meaning over decades of consumption
Shapes that take a backseat to their saccharine and more flamboyant foils

Even though it is they, with their oat colored simplicity,
Who somehow make the highly coveted, sticky confections all the more desirable

stuffed —FULL— OF— FRENCH FRIES & *sorrow*

Eat
by Lily LeFebvre

It's a sensation not worth having
The pain in the pit of your stomach
Somehow a relief flooding over
But your pant line ever demanding

First it started as a 'juice cleanse'
Then a fixation with the chill of ice
Now it's beyond counting calories
Stirring the concern of your friends

The white sheet like a butcher's shop
Greets you like the patient you are
With a plan in your hands
You leave but you don't want to stop

But they won't let you keep going
And that first taste on your tongue
That first bite after all this time
Even if at first it's 'just showing'

There's more relief in caving in
Than there is in starving the beast

CHAPTER TWO
fulfillment

The Bitterest Goodbye
by Cassandra Bankson and Rhea Smith

Why does it hurt?
Before, I was promised
'Happily Ever After'

                                      'Happily Ever After'
                                specifies not when, nor where

She was a flower
Not the kind
You steep in tea,

                              dry curled petals, angry thorns
                                      In her stem, retribution

I tried, nonetheless
and for this,
I have bitter water and naught else

                                  if this is what they call love
                                        know I prefer it alone

A year to the day.
Salad dressing, sexual tension.
Unexpected.

                                      Unintended. Nonetheless,
                                      Love is not ours to dictate.

She made a mess;
of promises made,
of my apartment, of my life

                                I can clear these walls of her
                                But she remains on my mind

Photo albums void of memories,
Matchbox, Shamrock,
Cards never sent.

                                    Bitterness behind her lips
                                Makes friendship a poker game

Relationships.
Not espionage.
This was not what I expected.

                                        Regretfully, these last sips
                                        Go down like too-harsh whiskey

Heavy breath,
I wish her all the best.
I forgive what there may be left.

                                        Not because she was right, but,
                                          Because I deserve freedom.

Because I deserve
a sweeter taste,
because I deserve something real;

                                            Because I *do* deserve it;
                                            Happily ever after.

feminism is fun

Natalie Meagan

My Selfish Muse
by Lily LeFebvre

I'm seeking my muse, she will'd not be found
Or at least, that's how it's starting to seem
From planting these seeds right into the ground,
From seeking these answers within my dreams

I've tried rum, I've tried gin, even whiskey
And the words that result are not wanted.
Now – here comes the part where I get frisky,
And now every second I am haunted.

Bending and moaning and seeking release,
And in that moment things seem to look up;
But just as fleeting – I flee from these sheets
And there! Find her waiting within my cup.

I curl up with tea and make my last plea
Just… please bring my happiness back to me.

Mantra
by Alyssa Paxson

Soften your gaze
Treat yourself as you would a child
Forgive yourself

Speak to yourself as kindly
As you would a friend

Focus on the good stuff
List them on lined journal pages
With a colorful gel pen

Savor the good things
Without waiting
For mythical perfection
No guilt

Don't dwell, stuck focusing on negatives
Look them over, but don't stay there for always

Set intentions
Small things count and multiply

Embrace your power
Use it for good
Redirecting negative spirals
Into hopeful leaps of faith

Alyssa Paxson

Blank page.
by Caz Brett

The blank page.
Blank. Totally, unapologetically blank.
Fingers hovering above the keys, waiting - just waiting - for something brilliant to type. You'd like to type something brilliant. Something meaningful, that people will look at approvingly and think "Yes! This is me!" or frown at whilst internalising a shout of "I disagree!" - or they will be so incredibly moved by the profanity of what you've written that they will cry; heavy, choking, nasty tears. Or silent deadly ones that will slide down their face uncontrollably and they'll hastily wipe away hoping nobody will notice.

The page is still blank.
You are hoping and willing for your brain to conjure up something so beautiful, something so brilliant.
Yet, inevitably, time goes on, and the page is still blank, still empty. You've got so much crammed in your head, but nothing wants to come out.

I remember a time when writing was a breeze. When I was seven, I fashioned a 'night torch pen', a tiny flashlight tied to a biro, which meant I could stay up until the small hours, scribbling away in one of the many notebooks I had at hand. All sorts of stories would pour out; tales of crazy Mayors, who only dressed in brown and held dinner parties for the local fishermen on a Tuesday, or stories of a cat that thought it was a fondant fancy. Half-written science-fiction novels that started with such vigour but ran out as soon as I realised I knew nothing about aeronautical engineering and that gravity was still a little bit of a puzzle to me. (I still to this day wonder how on earth the Millennium Falcon could come out of hyperspace into the area where

Alderaan was supposed to be, and somehow it automatically adjusted for the change in gravity without leaving them splatted against the back of the cabin. I can explain that one to you over a glass of wine if you'd like to discuss further. I am truly a delight at dinner parties.)

I was told off at school frequently for not paying attention – because I was reading ahead, or because I was secretly writing away under the desk. I wrote a six-part novel when I was nine about a haunted house, which was based on a school trip we'd been on when I was seven, and I was sent to the headmaster's office for not working. Instead, he read the entire thing over two hours (okay, six-part novella, if you will) whilst I sat outside writing in yet another notebook, convinced I was in trouble. Eventually he called me in, told me quietly that I was very talented, and he was happy to read any other stories I'd written.

I started a fantasy thriller when I was eleven. I submitted the first chapter – a graphic description of an elf being beheaded by a magician – into a competition for under-14s. It was, perhaps, a bit gory and in hindsight maybe a little more adult than the other entries might have been, but it was good enough to win. I got the impression that it blew most of the other entries completely out of the water. I had the story published, and was given an award, and I was incredibly proud of myself. I continued writing the fantasy thriller – in fact, I even rewrote and completely changed the first chapter. Award-winning or not, I had new ideas I wanted to inject into it. New characters, new approaches. I was buzzing with plotlines and imagined maps of this fantasy world I was creating.

If anyone was destined to spend the rest of their life writing, it was me. But did I? Absolutely not.

I can't even begin to work out what happened. I was bursting with stories, and then I just seemed to run into some trouble. I wrote poetry and songs at university, and tinkered about with a story - which I wrote a good 75,000 words of. Then about five years ago – I just ran out. It's like my brain just switched off. Am I an adult now? Was this inevitable? Or have I broken myself, somehow? And if I have, can I ever be repaired?

My fingers tentatively hover over the keys again. I have tried bringing it back, I have really, really tried. I've tried notebooks. I used to fill up hundreds of notebooks, with ideas or names or drawings of things that I liked. Now, I have hundreds of notebooks but they reflect what it feels like inside my head. They're just empty, waiting to be filled, sadly knowing that they never will.

My heart aches slightly as I'm writing this, because I know it to be true. I know it to be the saddest secret I ever had. I still habitually buy notebooks because I know I have the want to fill them, but they just pile up and up and up, and I'm thinking about how much I want to write but how little I have left to say. They will never be filled, and I will never be fulfilled. And that is why I will always be thinking about the blank page. I will always allow my fingers to hover above the keys, as I think about how much I want to say and how I just can't find the words to write.

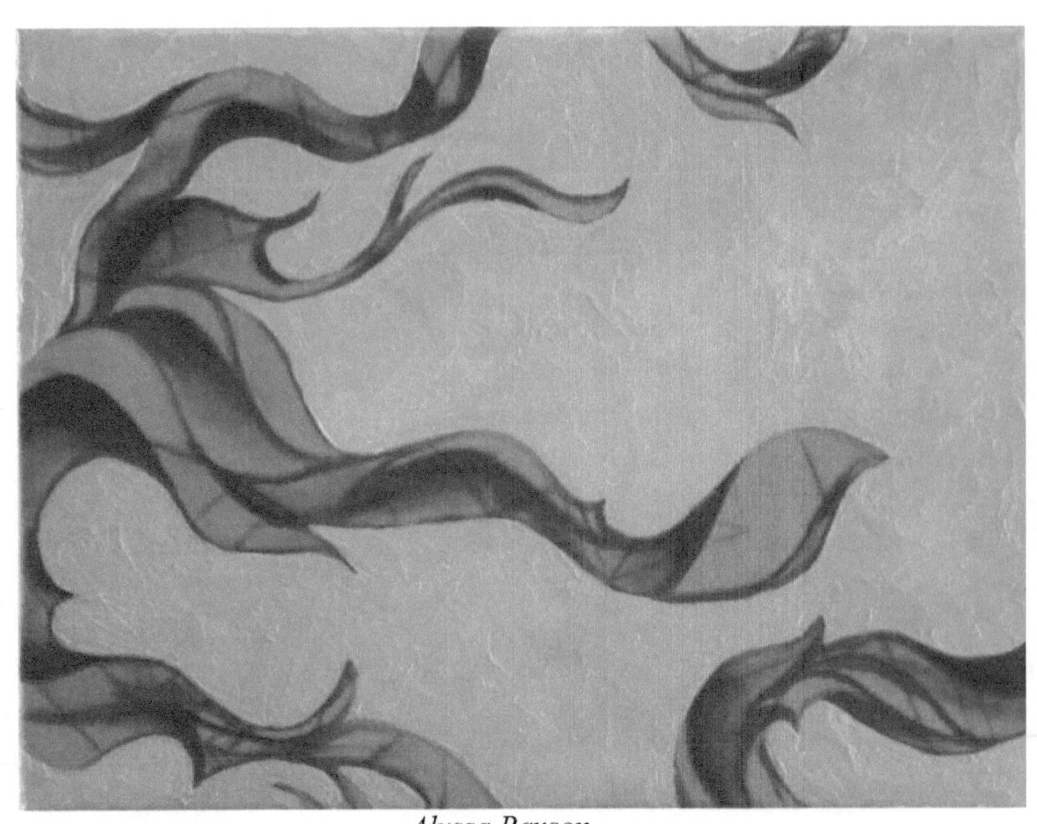
Alyssa Paxson

Disrupting the Image of Beauty
by Cassandra Bankson

Good morning, victim of circumstance.
Who does the world want you to be?
I'm exhausted with conforming and playing along;
What happened to what matters underneath?
Society has an obsession
With the image of perfection
Hide your truths inside
And loathe your own reflection
Emotions and opinions we are told not to mention
What a dejected existence...
Shouldn't beauty take a new direction?
Life gave me scars from battles won
Against myself and against the world
But the only remark from eyes that see
Call them "imperfections on a little girl".
These badges of beauty are only viewed
As the aftermath of mistakes
But they're tattoos with deeper stories
History, etched onto body and face.
Surgery, stitches, accidents, abuse,
Life lessons, and disease,
Our scars are proof of strength and hope,
Not marks that should displease.
If love is illegal, and beauty is defined
Through the pages of a magazine,
Where is the space, that's left behind
To love the authentic me?
Gender Identity,
Is seen as an obscenity,
And changing that would be "wrong",
But what happens when,

Deep within,
It's who you have been all along?
Transgender hearts, torn apart.
Identity crawling underneath the wrong skin.
They're laughing along,
But living alone,
When they're told to "hold it in".
Little boys who want Barbie dolls,
Or girls who feel best in briefs,
Live an existence that's inhospitable,
To who they are underneath.
Robots on a runway,
Size zeroes wait in line,
An industry that sets the rules,
To which beauty is defined.
Society is embellished with vast variety,
But the only parts that seem alright,
Are what's projected on a screen.
Too fat, too short, too tall, too thin,
We are up against a wall.
With all of these labels and stereotypes,
How can we feel beautiful at all?
Everyone's trying so hard to be everyone else,
But the pattern leaves no room,
To grow into ourselves.
These wings are marked with tears and holes,
But it's time to spread them wide:
To release the weights of judgment,
And remember
I can fly.
You can't constrict evolution,
Or construct a perfect being.
It's time to let color fill the void,

And accept who we are meant to be.
Graffiti on a comment wall,
Letters typed up on a screen.
We hashtag "Inner Beauty",
But do we know what it means?
The battle of beauty will surely rage on,
But the new definition is anything but wrong.
So lose the lure to conform,
Beauty is not blemish free.
These imperfections, and mistakes,
Give true beauty
Validity.

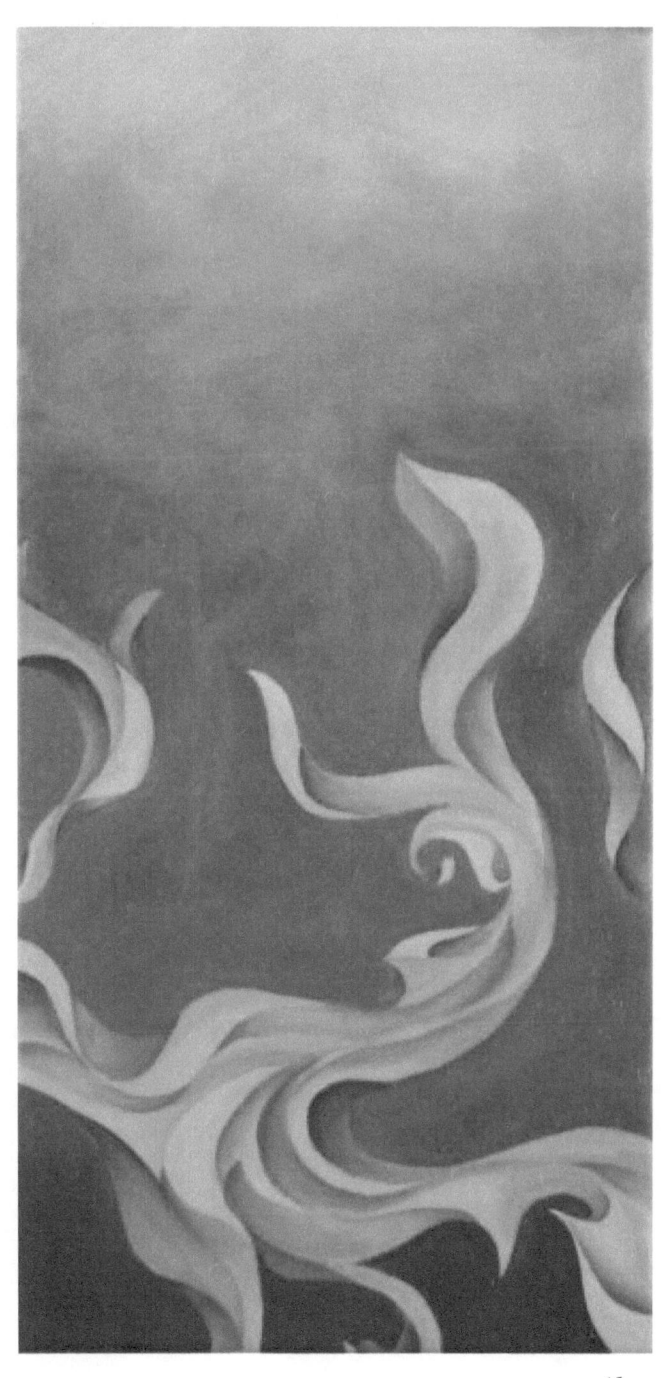

Alyssa Paxson

CHAPTER THREE
anxiety

Monsters
by Louisa Tracey

It used to sit in her wardrobe. The monster was there every night; she just knew it. She'd always make sure to slide the doors closed. Tight. If they were open a fraction she worried she might see it. See its eyes glowing in the dark. Watching. Waiting. For what? She wasn't sure. But it was always there.

She grew and aged and the monster wasn't hiding in storage any more. For a long time, it was forgotten about. An occasional twinge, a niggle. Some childhood memory that lingered but didn't frighten the same way.

When the monster returned, she didn't notice at first. It crept in quietly, usually at night. Followed her around when she left the house. She didn't notice, because it was invisible. She had feared seeing it so much in the dark, but she never could have. Now out in the open it could get close. It got bold enough to bring a friend who was heavy and liked to sit on her shoulders. They'd often whisper things in her ears. Sometimes they'd scream.

"You're worthless."

"Everything is dangerous."

"You're failing."

"Maybe we shouldn't leave the house today."

"No one cares."

She did everything she could to quiet the monsters who followed her around. But soon they became part of her. They were there every day.

Digging their claws in and feeding off of her. She accepted her fate, this was just how things would be.

Until one day, she saw someone else dragging a monster around. She couldn't see her own but others were so much more visible. She saw the burdens they carried and the hurt the monsters caused. Someone told her what her own monsters looked like and they started to show, like ships emerging from fog.

Now she sees her monsters as clear as day. She faces them head on, fights with them, screams back when their bawling becomes unbearable. Sometimes the monsters overwhelm, they scare her and she retreats. But the more she fights, the more she helps others with their monsters, the smaller hers seem to get. They've shrunk. They still hang around and she supposes they always will, but she's learning their weaknesses and knows they'll never truly win.

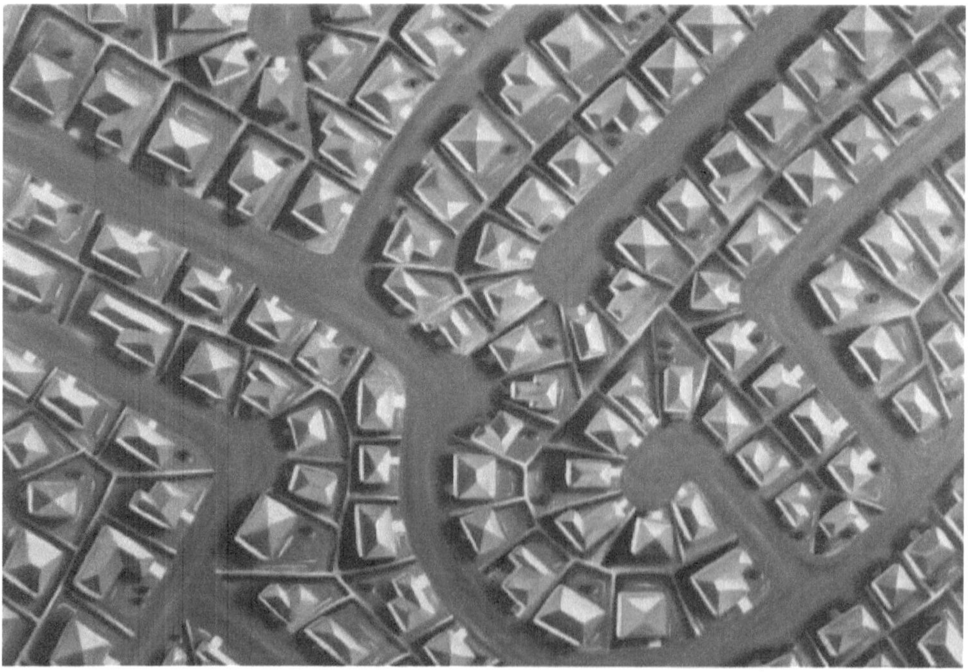

Alyssa Paxson

Numbers
by Cassandra Bankson

A state of tranquil anxiety;
The kind where you sit still and feel your muscles shake,
Your heart palpitates.
Smile corners soft,
Breathing stern.
A hospital waiting room,
The leaser's chair at a bank.
Cardiac transplants or credit scores,
Numbers matter.
But you can always bend the rules,
Abundance flows like blood through you.

But Did I?
by Rebecca Foley

Climbing into bed with my "Walking Dead" pajamas on, I set my phone's alarm for 8:30am, 8:45am, 9:00am, and 9:30am. I place my phone face down on my bedside table, lay my head on my pillow, and close my eyes.

Sleep here I come. Did I set my alarm? Yeah I know I did. But did I? I reach for my phone and check. *Alarm set. It's 11:10 now. Did I study enough for my exam? Am I going to fail? What are the ancestors of science fiction? Romance. Travel narrative. Utopia Fiction. Two more. What are they? If you can't remember you're going to fail! Gothic! And, and, THE EPIC! What if I can't remember them tomorrow? What if I can't remember anything? What if I don't wake up on time? What if I'm late and miss my exam? Wake up at 8:30. Wake up at 8:30. Did I set my alarm?* I reach for my phone and check. *Alarm is set. It's 11:15 now. I should stop telling people about all the TV shows I watch. They probably think I'm a sad lonely human being. Which is the truth. I'm going to be alone forever. Did I set my alarm? You did. You did. You don't need to look.* I reach for my phone and check. *Alarm is definitely set. It's 11:30 now. Why can't I speak in class? Am I going to get enough participation points? Am I going to fail my classes? I know I set my alarm, but did I?* I reach for my phone and check. *Alarm is still set for 8:30am. It's midnight now. I need to sleep, but what if I sleep and I sleep through my alarm? I don't want to go to class tomorrow. I'm going to fail. Did I set my alarm…*

SHIT SHIT SHIT SHIT SHIT SHIT
HIT SHIT SHIT SHIT SHIT SHIT SH
T SHIT SHIT SHIT SHIT SHIT SHIT
SHIT SHIT SHIT SHIT SHIT SHIT
HIT SHIT SHIT SHIT SHIT SHIT SH
T SHIT SHIT SHIT SHIT SHIT SHIT
SHIT SHIT SHIT SHIT SHIT SHIT
HIT SHIT SHIT SHIT SHIT SHIT SH
T SHIT SHIT SHIT SHIT SHIT SHIT
SHIT SHIT SHIT SHIT SHIT SHIT
HIT SHIT SHIT SHIT SHIT SHIT SH
T SHIT SHIT SHIT SHIT SHIT SHIT
SHIT SHIT OH. WAIT. NO. IT'S FINE.

Natalie Meagan

The Morning After
by Cassandra Bankson

Fingerprints of dew, born from 8 hours of night sweats and respiration clung to my windows like tiny crystals, glimmering with the remnant hope I held to so tightly the night before.

I woke up in a nightmare this morning, eyelashes hanging like heavy curtains, soaked with saline tears of discrimination, repression, and pain.

Late Tuesday night, in the hours that the threat of Wednesday began to rear its head, [he] had acquired the title of "President" through a political system almost as flawed as the minds of his supporters.

A feeling of disgust and uncertainty mixed together in my esophagus in a way that no flu shot could prevent.

Heavy morning air swam into my lungs and expanded like a pufferfish inside the ribbed hull of my chest, lifting my collarbones on a wave of inhalation to kiss my chin.

My tongue was parched and numb to the point that I could feel the cracks between my own taste buds; my mind as blank as a canvas, and my heart felt as if it had been paralyzed by Novocaine.

Standing was a bad idea; I was a tower of Jenga blocks swaying with the hazard of toppling over, mirroring the current state of a severed America.

Thoughts flitted through my mind like a leaf falling in your peripheral vision, always too insignificant to notice and too quick to catch. Engravings of feelings were carved into my person the way lovers' initials scar the steadfast trunks of trees, but my current state of stinging shock and disbelief wouldn't allow my mind to focus on anything other than the hollow alabaster wall.

Rose was out of the country on a soul-searching trip, dancing across the ancient mosaic stones of Barcelona, and to my heart's protest I hoped she stayed there. Even in my crypt of apathy, this realization shocked me enough to suspend my jaw like a drawbridge.

Only days before my laughter had rippled through her hair like the wind, but now there is no reason for her to return here. Love is blind, and I'd rather she continue gallivanting blissfully across the Spanish countryside, throwing those ribbons of hair so wildly over her shoulder.

Am I awake?
America are you awake?
Time today seems to eat at the blood in my veins the way antidepressants do.
How do I get through today?
How do we get through the next four years?
I've spent the last 23 of them fighting myself relentlessly.
What does this mean for me?
What does this mean for us as a nation?
Worst case scenario, Finnish winters can be fought with multiple layers of wool.

Wool, so similar to my warm cocoon of stitched and woven comfort, beckoning me to hibernate and rest my heavy heart and lethargic mind into its waves of lulling cotton thread counts.

Is this caffeine withdrawal, shaking my bones like piano keys do their strings? A cortisol response, chemically repressing my ability to function? Has the carcass of depression I buried a year ago found a holy revival?

Even the twilight of soft dawn was overwhelming as it cut through my eyelids with a sharpened edge – the silence intoxicating to the point of suffocation – all I wanted to do was escape, riding the saddle of thoroughbred sleep.

Nothing my mind could conjure up could be worse than living this nightmare.

The Duality of Anxiety
by Meg Colt

Panic you are my norm,
I feel confused without you.
But yet I'm disoriented with you.

There are pills that ebb your presence,
blue ones,
white ones,
colorful ones.
But when you aren't here,
I'm almost incomplete.

Anxiety you are an odd creature,
a stranger whispering to me,
the opposite of a best friend or confidant.

You are the bully that tormented me in school,
the step-parent that abused me,
the friend I thought I could trust,
who stabbed me in the back instead.

Ahh good old anxiety,
causing me to worry when I should be playing,
making my throat dry
and my hands tremble.
Good old anxiety,
making a fool of me when I should be casual.

But dear old friend,
what am I without you?
Are you a part of me,
am I a part of you?

Have you always been here?
Can we ever peacefully coexist?

You might make me who I am,
but also drain me completely.
What kind of relationship is this?

Each day I push you away,
I shove you hard.
You've left me scarred,
no respect, no regard.

But finally there has come a day,
a day I can start anew.
I'm cutting you off dear anxiety,
right where you grew.
At last you've deserted me,
with not even a call on the phone.

Finally, someplace I can be alone.

The Fight
by Hannah Maine

I wake up later than I'd like and think, "You have to get up and do…" But I come up short. "What do I have to get up for?" And with that question remaining unanswered, I pull together the little willpower my restless sleep left me with and drag myself out of bed for no other reason than the little joy I find in coffee.

I plop myself in front of the one sight that will fill the majority of my day—my glowing computer screen. The bold subjects of emails shout importance, but hold no substance inside. I sort through the meaningless content to get it out of the way and find when I'm finished, two hours have somehow passed by.

More time passes as I go through the motions. I switch from the screen of my computer to the screen of my phone, scrolling through social media. I open Instagram countless times, escaping in the pretty pictures and perfect lives of other people. For a few moments, I feel satisfied by the aesthetic beauty and success of others. But the secondhand fulfillment is accompanied by ruthless comparison and self-loathing: "See—that person actually does something with herself" or "You can never be successful because you have no talent and don't work hard."

The day passes slowly, yet is over suddenly. I feel as though my brain never even woke up. "What did I even do today?" I ask myself. The answer is nothing. But I quickly brush past the thought, busying my hands and mind with idle tasks, pushing past the sick feeling in my stomach and tightening in my chest. I am clinging desperately onto the thin door of distraction to keep my cruel thoughts at bay.

The feeling of dread always lurks beneath the surface. Every happy moment, watching TV or going on a walk, is accompanied by the negative thoughts, hanging over my head, just waiting for the inevitable idle moment where they can fill my attention and wrap me in an anxious spiral.

I hold on with all of my might. Trying so hard to ignore the tightness in my chest as I smile at my boyfriend over dinner. Trying to enjoy the good pieces of my life I have been given. But my throat tightens regularly and the smallest things remind me that I will have to face my demons soon.

I know it's coming, but I am not prepared. I have no solutions prepared, no tactics that successfully silence the voice in my head. I have not gotten anywhere in my attempts to find adequate answers to the sharp, hateful questions my mind barks at me at night. But the time for sleep approaches and after hours of Netflix shows filling the space in my brain, I resign. I must spend time alone in my head.

Although my sweet boy has been sleeping soundly next to me for hours, I lay wide awake. I am not only far from sleep; I am more awake than I have been all day. Adrenaline has filled my body, and I feel like I need to run a marathon to get out all the energy. However, it is late, so I lay in bed and let my mind run on instead.

"What are you doing with your life?" it asks me. "Why are you here?" "Why can't you figure this out?" I hear my own voice spit at me with disgust.

Every problem in my life comes to the surface and my mind demands they all be solved. Now.

"You don't do anything all day. How is it possible you can't even write a blog post for months?"

"You graduated from a top college and went on to do nothing. This is what you got your degree for? Why can't you do something successful and impressive like everyone else who went to your school?"

"Why don't you make more money? You need to find a way to make more money to pay your credit card bill. Even more, you need to make more money to pay for more so your boyfriend can be less stressed. You bring nothing to the table. Why would anyone want you around?"

"You are nothing." My mind tells me, and my heart aches in defeat.

After hours of being beat relentlessly, I am saved by my physical exhaustion and drift off. However, in my sleep, I continue to fight with my mind inside of the stress dreams that mirror reality, or my fear-clouded perception of reality, far too accurately.

I wake up cold, yet damp all over from my sweat. After fighting my way through another night, it's time to face the day.

"Get up. You're so lazy. You can't just stay in bed all morning." And it begins again.

Acai Violetta
by Lily LeFebvre

I'm not ruined
I'm just ruminating
On some things that went so wrong
I'm not waiting,
I'm so tired of waiting,
Tired of waiting so long.
I'm not ruined,
I'm just ruminating
On - they said, they said I don't belong
To this life, I thought I said it's alright.

I'm not ruined, you've got it wrong.
I'm not ruined, you just put it off too long.

I'm not fading, it's just blue skies
Through red eyes I see
When it's violet,
It's all violence toward me
And I know, I know...
You'll show, you'll show.

I'm not ruined, despite ruminating;
And I'm not bitter, despite those days you left me to see
Just how cruel you were to me.

Chelsea Lewis for 'Anxiety Attack'

Anxiety Attack
by Rhea Smith

Left atrium. Flush.
Blinking, blood rush.
Center of the atrium, center of the crowd.
Center of my mind, thoughts screaming loud.
Flushing, rushing, beating faster,
this is my body, I am not master,
Fighting, losing, breath in all gasps
Cold sweat between fingers caught in clasps
All of these thoughts in the blink of an eye
People will stare, myself, I cry
I push through and all I see
A tunnel just for me
And all these people
Crowding
My space
Leave

Kayley Mills

CHAPTER FOUR
self-care

Kayley Mills

To My Younger Me
by Eileen Ramos

When you don't see yourself anywhere: …on any front covers, leads, commercials, the radio, bylines, love poetry, etc…

Do not believe you're unworthy for any screen or any page or any love letter.

Do not disappear due to their neglect.

It's hard to see yourself as beautiful, when everyone adores the individuals who look nothing like you. Not even in your so-called homeland, with their casts full of long and narrow faces, white skin, big eyes, and pointy noses. Not with their lithe and tall bodies.

Look at the mirror. I know you hate it. But look. Gaze into your eyes. Smile at your vessel. Know that you're alive, breathing, and experiencing the world through your wondrous perspective.

Touch your skin. Graze your fingers across your brown surface. Experience every oil, each grease spot, your hair no matter how oily or tough it is. Every pimple, every bump, every scar. Whether you feel your ribs or rolls of fat. Whether you have a hairy upper lip or a unibrow,

You. Are. So. Amazing. If they don't place you within the spotlight, write those stories yourself.

You can become the protagonist, the heroine. The center of a love triangle. The slayer of all demons (your demons). You can save the day, even the entire world. You can be the detective, the whistleblower. You can be the brilliant inventor, the rising star onstage, and so much more.

You can be more than your stereotype, the model (and invisible) minority. In fact you already are. You don't have to believe what the media tells you. What society tells you either.

You'd hate your entire being if you fell for their lies. They don't represent you. Therefore they don't deserve you.

Look at that mirror again. And right into your eyes. The only person you need to love is yourself. Not this fool's gold made up of airbrushing, photoshopping, and hella good lighting. You're more real than any Chanel commercial. More genuine than any manic pixie dream white girl.

Your every breath is you shining. Your every smile rightfully earns our standing ovation. Your tight hold onto your identity is more valuable than the Eurocentric beauty ideals they shove.

Defy them. Do what you can to hold onto your innate wonder. Don't let them whitewash and degrade who you are.

You're too lovely to give up on, so turn off the TV. Throw away that tacky fashion magazine. And open your notebook to a blank page, and show us what beauty truly looks like.

Caroline Linford

Wash Our Hands I
by Kaitlyn Luckow

You kissed his lips
and tangled the
webs between your feet.
but there's a need to open
your eyes
to become less asleep
and a need to swim up
to breathe again,
and reclaim the air
you gave to his lips.

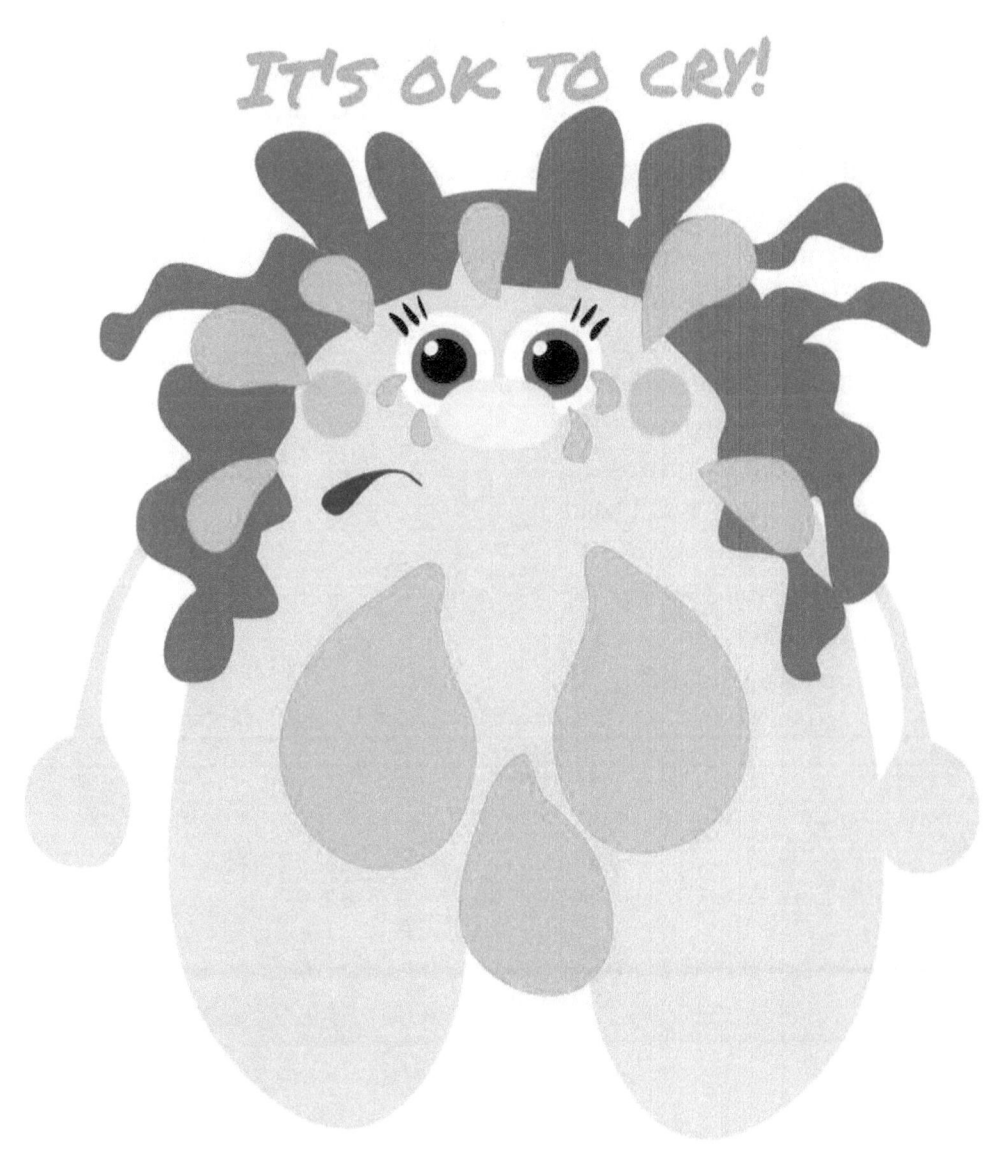

Caroline Linford

self-love
by Haley Littlefield

self-love is not selfish
it is your first defense against the world
you can forge an impenetrable armor
through your willingness to put yourself first
no, self-love is not selfish
but it is defiant
to tell the world you will not be beaten
you will not be torn down
for you are an iron fortress
built up by your own full heart
self-love is not selfish
it is an act of true courage
a show of strength and grace
when you love yourself
no one can hurt you

Caroline Linford

Wash Our Hands II
by Kaitlyn Luckow

Speak to the winds
of tides crashing down
the unheard whispers
of yesterday.
Put the words on the
backs of wings
and let them
        Rise Up.

I MAY CRY BUT I CAN STILL GET THINGS DONE.

To Care For Me
by Alyssa Paxson

Holding you close
'Til you're sleeping soundly.
Gently untangling myself
Quietly climbing out of bed.
The baby monitor humming
Beneath the studio lamp's warm glow.

Taking the time
I know I need.
To do little things
to care for me.

Time on my yoga mat
In silence.
A few moments journaling
Or writing letters to friends.
Listening to music, sometimes dancing.
Watching a movie or a show.
Embroidering or crocheting.

Remembering just to breathe.
Letting my mind wander
Where it may.
Before finally making my way back
To the sweetest snuggles and dreams.

Kayley Mills

CHAPTER FIVE
mental health

Losing My Mind
by Cassandra Bankson

The insincere scent of antiseptics
Their latex greetings
Precautionary hygiene
It's not as morbid as you would think
Code blues are whisked away before they have a chance to decay
and spread their somber attitudes

A gurney is only a coffin on wheels
And she was the bloom you'd lay across my casket
The binge to my purge
The blood to my blade
Grotesque fantasies dancing behind a smile
A cerebral connection I refused to acknowledge or omit

Paint me a picture:
Sparkling white walls and lavish blue attire
5 star meals on the French Riviera
Servants at a call's command
I am the king of this castle.

A keyhole to reality:
Hysteria and propaganda
Rooms with one way locks
With phone notifications more important than med calls
It's no wonder we are delusional
Living under the veil of a forebrain fantasy
It's the only way to survive this nightmare.

No matter how many pills you swallow
This place in and of itself is a dopamine deficiency
A hotel for the hopeless

Built on a foundation of acetylcholine
With beds of benzodiazepines
See how well you sleep with Prozac as a pillow.

The cocktails they serve are expensive
Insured or out of pocket
But will also cost you a tax of tremors
And a slew of side effects

The nurse recognized my name and asked why I was here
Perplexed
Until she saw my legs.

Funny things happen when you don't eat,
don't sleep,
overthink,
cut too deep.

But it's all in your mind.
Or whatever you're lucky enough to have left of it.

Sexual assault in the psych ward,
The icing on the cake.

The Ativan in the needle,
The cortisol in the veins,
The Dilaudid down the hatch,
The morphine that drives one insane.

"Nurse, please wait!"

I'm a doctor, not a disaster.
I don't belong here.

Morning cannot be restrained and light will always shine through the darkness.

@kimmykeepr

Stigma
by Meg Colt

Its grip is unyielding, it's often paralyzing
It is a cumbersome burden, far more than any boulder
It causes the mind to never cease analyzing
It is a pint-sized evil resting on the shoulder

Sometimes it's incredibly controlling,
unfortunately more often than not
The barrage of worry is endlessly patrolling
and like a deer in the headlights you're caught

It is intangible to others, it cannot be seen
but for the sufferer never out of mind
For this ailment there is no vaccine
but its victims end up resigned

As long as the universal stigma carries on
This mental illness will carry its baton

Train Tracks
by Lily LeFebvre

I have somewhere to be. I'm probably going to be late, realistically. Yet here I am again, no train in sight, and I'm zoning out on those grimy, well-worn metal tracks. As usual, the same thoughts are running through my mind.

I should probably stop here before I continue, just to get one thing straight – I'm not suicidal. I like my life. At least, I like it well enough. And the thought of thoughts ending – just stopping – a total abyss, scares the ever-living hell out of me. And the pain – there's no way to know if death hurts. You can't exactly ask the dead, can you?

But ever since I was a little girl, I've always had these thoughts. I'll stare at these train tracks and think – What if I just did it? What if I stepped off this platform, and let myself fall? Would I die that horrible death that they warn you the third rail will bring upon you? Would I touch it and instantly be singed from head to toe, emitting the god-awful stench of burning flesh? Or would I survive the fall, and just lay there until the next train came? Would that be it for me? Would it run over my legs first, or smash into my head and break my spine in an instant?

All the while, these questions are accompanied by vivid, almost too real images and sensations of what each would actually look or feel like. It terrifies me to my core. Surely 'normal' folk don't contemplate their demise during their down time. Do they? I find it hard to believe that they do. Especially from such a young age.

I can remember needing to leave the room during a horror film because of a torture scene. All I could keep thinking about was if it had been me getting paper cuts forcibly applied up and down my legs. Hell, even now it gives me shivers throughout my spine to think about. Surely that can't be a normal occurrence. Some folks might call it empathy, and I suppose in that situation it makes sense. But can that really be what you'd call my constant imagining of the moment of my death every single time I approach these tracks?

I think I think too much.
        They're just train tracks after all.
            My train is here.

Natalie Meagan

There is a Monster in All of Us
by Lucy Ellerton

There is a monster in all of us. We may never have a reason to set it free, or to let it control our lives – but it is there. One day there will be a trigger, a spark. Someone or something will trip that wire and you will be aware of your monster's existence.

My realization came when I was 15. My parents had gone out and I had been left alone to babysit my brother who was 11 at the time. I was a child pretending to be an adult, the using the authority that the title 'babysitter' implied. I was in charge. I dictated what we did and I was to be obeyed. But 11 year olds don't always obey those in authority – especially if that person in authority is their older sibling.

The first time he baulked, I insulted him.

The second time he did not do as he was told, I yelled at him.

The third time… the third time – the monster came out.

My pride was stung, my ego was hurt, and my anger was strong. So, I hit him. I hit him again and again and again. Not strong enough to do any harm, but strong enough to be mildly painful.

I was immediately horrified by what I had done. He was crying, I was crying – I don't know which of us felt worse. I dragged him to our back door – to push him away, to keep him safe from the uncontrollable thing I had become. But my parents got home before he was even outside.

So, I ran.

I just left, wearing only my school uniform and socks. I just couldn't face them; I couldn't even face myself. I wandered my suburb's streets like that for hours, my feet freezing cold. I even got on a train in a vain effort to try and get some sleep but the neon lights were too bright and I could not collect any sort of comfort.

The end of this story comes from the kindness of one person. I never knew his name, but he recognized that I was running from something and decided to help. He saw me trying to sleep on a cold train platform with some old newspapers on my feet for warmth. He came to talk to me and he offered me some money for a phone call so I could get someone to come get me. The he offered me a bed for the night "no questions asked" – even offering to bring his girlfriend to the station so that I may feel safe.

I decided to take the phone call.

That night could have ended so differently if it had not been for this person. He could have been a murderer, a rapist or a thief. But he wasn't and he saw the goodness in me and not the evil I was running from.
I went home, I slept, I apologized and was forgiven - I even eventually forgave myself.
I know there is a monster inside of me, that there is a potential for evil. But it is now behind bars, trapped in a cage and I will do everything in my power to keep it there forever.

Everyone has a monster but mostly it is caged and hidden behind kindness, compassion and understanding. That nameless man helped me cage my monster and I will do as much as I can to help everyone else who needs help do the same.

Medicated
by Lily LeFebvre

Some pills to keep me down,
Some pills to perk me up.
Some pills to hold my tongue,
And pills to spill my guts.
These pills keep me alive,
Or functional at least.
Aren't they the same to us?
Some day I'll live pill free.
That day is not today,
Not with my mind still healing.
Some pills keep me alive,
When I need to stop the feelings.

Alyssa Paxson

The Fight
by Rebecca Foley

The sun rises up in the early morning sky, shining through the blinds with such force. When I open my eyes, I see him. He is on top of me, laying on my chest, holding me down. Air is hard to breathe through the diaphragm. Up and down motions of the stomach, compressed by him.

I try to sit up, but I'm pushed back down as if I have been pinned to a brick wall by a semi-truck. His small furry paw is more powerful than expected. Why is there a black and white cat on my chest? I try to push him off, but his claws dig into me, leaving marks and cuts and scratches that bleed. On my abdomen, where no one will see. The cat glares at me, telling me that I can't get up. I try with all my might to resist the cat's piercing gaze and insistent hisses. He digs deeper. His reassuring meows are too strong, I cannot resist. I gaze into his eyes, feeling the energy pulled from deep inside. I don't want to move. I just want to lay in bed. *Forever.*

I'm about to close my eyes again when I feel the weight released from my chest. I can once again breathe with ease. A dog with a golden coat has pounced and thrown the cat across the room. Looking over, I see the cat lying in the far dark corner, the one spot in my room where the sun cannot reach. He shivers with pain and hisses under his breath. The dog stands between me and the cat, baring its pearly white teeth and growling. Her teeth are rather shiny for a dog. Her golden coat glistens in the sun's rays. She turns around just enough to keep one eye on me and the other on the pile of quivering fur in the corner. She gestures to the right. Not wanting to take my eyes off the intense scene but intrigued by what she wants, I look around. I notice that my room is quite bare. There are no posters on the walls, no pictures on the mantel, not even a rug on the floor. After a moment of hesitation, I notice my bathroom door is open.

Just as I turn towards the door, I hear a high pitched yelp. Slowly turning around, I see the nails of the cat jammed inside the dog's skin. He pulls bits of fur from her back. The left paw first pulls out a clump, then the right, then the back paws, as if he were trying to find a comfortable place to lay down. The eyes of the dog look deep into mine, pleading for me to save myself. The cat whips his head around and scowls at me. There is nowhere to hide, but the bathroom.

I race to the bathroom, the cat on my tail. I slam the door closed, locking him out. Sitting on the side of the bathtub, I notice the floral walls, which were decorated by the previous tenant, who must have been obsessed with flowers and cheery colors. The walls all throughout the apartment were bright yellows. These walls make me want to vomit. Did the yellow walls bring that miserable cat? No. This cat would hate bright colors. Blues and soft grays would bring him. How do I know this? And why is there a cat in my room? If the yellows didn't bring the cat, did it bring the dog? Her polished coat matches the walls almost perfectly. I feel her nuzzle her head beneath my hand. *So soft, so perfect, so…*

I quickly look up towards the closed door and right in front of it stands the cat, glaring at me with its one dark green eye and one murky yellow. He skulks closer and closer, the soft fur of the dog gone. I slide back as far as I can go, falling into the tub. Grabbing the shower head, I spray water at him, trying to fend him off, but nothing is working. He skulks closer and closer, his eyes set on me. He pounces and clings to my chest. The left paw scratches, the right paw pierces, the left cuts, the right… The right is pulled away as if he's going to swiftly take off my face, but he doesn't. He looks me dead in the eye and I see it.

One claw extends from the paw, reaches towards my right forearm and slices upward. Blood pours from the wound, filling the bathtub with warm liquid. I feel the pulse inside me quicken and slow. I blink and the cat is gone. Quickly surveying the bathroom, looking for him, but he is nowhere. As I survey the room, I notice that the walls aren't that hideous, but actually quite lovely. I look in the mirror that hangs above the sink, it's cracked. A piece of the glass is missing from the corner. Through the steamed surface I see my face. Tears flow slowly down my once flush cheeks. My face turning ghost white, as the blood drains from my face and escapes my body. My eyes slowly look downward and widen. The glass shard rests in my left hand. I close my eyes, slowly.

A warm, wet, breathy sensation occurs over my blood-soaked arm. Something rough and stubbly rubs against me. I open my eyes slightly, just enough to see a slimy pink tongue licking the blood around my wound. She is trying to help. The dog is trying to make up for failing me. The corners of my mouth turn up a little. I glance down, past my dripping forearm and see that the bubble bath mat is pooling with blood. The bath mat that once looked like a sheet of bubble wrap, now looks like red polka dots. I can't keep my eyes open anymore. I close them slowly, hearing a distant whimper. I don't know if it's from me or the dog.

It seems so quiet, at first. There's beeping and footsteps and talking. Where am I? Weights are pushing hard on my head and eyes. I force my eyes open and all I see is white, bright white. I miss my yellow walls. My vision blurs and my head pounds. I'm about to close my eyes when I realize something. Where are my yellow walls? I spring forward, into a sitting position, but I am yanked back down by constraints on my arms. I'm trapped, with nowhere to hide. He's going to get me! The cat's going to get me! I close my eyes and weep.

"Miss." I hear a deep voice call out. It's a struggle to lift my eyelids enough to see the tall figure standing over me. "You're in the hospital. You've lost a lot of blood. You must have someone looking out for you." I just stare at the man in the white lab coat. "I'll let you rest," he says and walks out.

I'm about to close my eyes for the last time, when I hear a muffled whine. I look over to the far corner of the hospital room and see a golden shimmer. She sits in the corner with such prestige. The golden dog walks forward. I realize that inside her mouth is the black and white cat. She drops the motionless cat in the trash can next to the door, bares her teeth at me as if to smile, and walks over to me. She licks the bandage around my arm. I notice that the cat peeks out of the trash can, just from the eyes up. It feels as if the cat is the predator and I am his prey and he is waiting for the perfect time to pounce. The dog whips her head around and growls at the cat, who falls back into the trash can.

I am released from the hospital a couple days later. The nurse wheels me out in a wheelchair, the dog on my lap. Every once in a while she will growl behind me, keeping the cat at bay. At home, I grow to love the yellow walls and their insanely cheerful floral pattern. Every night my dog climbs in bed with me and keeps the cat from climbing on top of me. The cat sulks in the corner, where the sun doesn't touch, and waits. Every once in awhile, he will creep closer and I will feel my chest tighten, but whenever this happened, my dog nudges my hand with her muzzle. As I pet her soft fur, I look into her eyes. I see a sparkle and just know. I will never close my eyes again.

Alyssa Paxson

CHAPTER SIX
love

He Is Music
by Haley Littlefield

The sound of his voice is my greatest discovery.
He speaks to me and only me.
It is mine. His words echo from the bottom of my soul and resonate within my heart.
He is my great symphony creating frisson and rebounding melodies that no ears could possibly be lucky enough to hear.
Yet, I do.
It is pure happiness. He is my love.

Unicorn's Pain and The Heart
by Rebecca Foley

Pearl white skin. Perfect white hair, flowing through the wind, lightly grazing the skin. Bright blue eyes peeking through the hair as it caresses the face. An ivory horn sticking out of the forehead, glistening in the sun's rays. A twinkle can be heard as each ray bounces off the horn. This is what a magnificent creature would look like if it weren't lying dead on the forest floor.

A unicorn lays motionless. Hornless. Bloodless. The unicorn had been slaughtered by hunters looking for a quick buck. Taking the horn and draining the blood. The horn catches a mighty price, to the right buyer, while the blood has magical properties. If the blood is drunk right after death, but before the horn is extracted it can provide riches. If drunk after the horn is extracted, then the blood can provide beauty. If placed inside a cellar or another dark, damp place and drunk when one is about to die it can heal and give more years.

The best way to use unicorn blood is with the horn, though not many people know this. Grinding up the tip of the glistening horn right after the sun's rays hit the spiral and causes it to twinkle, then sprinkling it inside the blood, one can live forever. This may seem like a lot of extra work considering one can drink the blood before they die and gain more years, but gaining more years before a death can only give you at most 10 more years, sometimes not even that, and it can only be used once.

Once your extra years are up, Death approaches for real this time. Dressed in his black cloak - or so you would think. This ensemble is only for those that do not piss Death off by living longer than he allotted. No, Death will come to you as your worst fear and make you bow down to him and plead for mercy. If you're terrified of snakes, he will appear as a cobra; if you're terrified of spiders, he will appear as a tarantula; and if you're terrified of bugs, he will appear as a grasshopper with broken wings and slimy skin. If your pleading is adequate, he will kill you quickly, but if he is not satisfied he will punish you. Punish you severely and endlessly. This punishment will not only be for living too long but also for killing his favorite companion.

Unicorns were brought onto this Earth for Death's pleasure. Before Death existed, Chaos ruled the earth. People fought and fought, becoming mortally wounded but never dying. Chaos grew bored of the people healing and created Death from the bones of the wounded. Death swept the Earth, killing the wounded. This gave Chaos great pleasure. God and the Devil were also pleased, for Death brought the good and the evil to their rightful places. The good soared into the sky to the clouds above and the evil sunk into the ground to the flames below. The two were so eternally grateful that they came together and bestowed, upon Death, the unicorns. The unicorns had great beauty but with great beauty comes great greed.

Death became bonded to the unicorns. When they hurt, he hurts; and when they are happy, he is happy. They were connected in all ways. When Death is not killing off people, when their time has come, he watches the unicorns peacefully roam the earth. He can hear their thoughts; they thank him for his great pride in them. Their horns make the most wonderful music; the tune changing every day as the sun's rays become harsher or covered by clouds or shine through rain. These beautiful creatures are Death's beloveds. Once he even fell in love with one, but sadly it could not be for he was Death and one touch from his fleshless hand and death would follow.

This unicorn had beauty above the rest. Its hair was the perfect white of all the rest, but it had a shimmer of hope and wisdom. There were streaks of baby pink and lavender in the mane and even one streak of pale blue down the center of its tail. The unicorn's skin shined brighter than all the rest, more perfect than perfect and had a reflective glint to it. The horn dazzled and glistened far superior to the ordinary unicorn. But best of all this unicorn didn't praise and thank Death for taking pride in the unicorns, it took pride in him. He did the world a wonderful deed of bringing death to those in need. When the suffering becomes unbearable, Death is there. When the wounds hurt too much and the blood seeps out, Death is there. He protected the unicorns the best he could: even when he failed to save one of them, he didn't let it go unpunished.

Unicorns may seem like forgiving creatures but hurt one of their own and they will desolate. Unicorns physically cannot harm a living soul for they are God's creatures but they can hold a grudge for they are also the Devil's creatures. Death can hear this. With the need to protect the unicorns, his prized beings, plus the grudges they hold, he causes immense pain.

Death fell in love with the unicorn who had such great pride for him. He brought it berries, sugar, carrots, jelly beans, and of course the hearts of those that had killed the unicorn kind. Not once did Death touch the unicorn's perfect mane or skin. He never once touched its mouth when he fed it the gifts he brought. One day, he made the mistake. He fell so deep in love that when he was feeding the unicorn with the perfect skin, he touched the perfect hair. The unicorn instantly froze, eyes wide open, and turned to dust.

Death was devastated. So much anger and regret bubbled inside him. He wished he could kill himself, but Death cannot kill Death. He stayed far away from the other unicorns, afraid of accidently touching them. Even though one of their own died by Death's hand, they did not blame him. They still thanked him and wanted to be near him, but he just couldn't. He grew so depressed and frustrated that he killed as many people as he could. The Bubonic Plague ensued.

This didn't please Death. He grew tired of killing all these innocent lives. His heart was broken the day he killed the unicorn he loved. Ever since Death stopped killing all those random people and realized what was truly hurting him - his broken heart - he began killing those who had had their heart broken. If the break was deep enough, Death would release them from their pain.

Natalie Meagan

Stale Breadcrumbs
by Alyssa Paxson

Trying to retain my grip
On my tender center
Keep the walls from hardening around
Keep the prickly spikes
From coming to protect and punish
Protest the cold thoughtless
Words thrown at my core

How can I trust now
With how deeply you've bruised
Me at my most vulnerable
When I thought you'd be there
Surely
You were gone
Replaced with someone I don't recognize
Didn't realize you were leaving until he appeared
Begged him to bring you back

All these years I've begged
But the feeling has crept in
Compassion and understanding
Some things you'll always lack

Faith and hope alone can't keep love alive
And the breadcrumbs you drop
To string me along
Are growing so very stale

Gunpowder Hearts I
by Kaitlyn Luckow

I was in love
with your brick walls
obsessively trying to
grip on
and tear down,
but it just scraped
the skin of my hands
until I couldn't even
keep my grip on myself.

Puppy Love
by Rebecca Foley

good morning kisses
afternoon hugs
nighttime snuggles and cuddles
moonlit walks
Everything a girl could ask for
all wrapped up in one

Everything you do
For me you come to me
when I'm hurt and sad
wiping salty tears away
when I'm scared
protecting me and sending them away

my head buried in your chest
when I need a cry or
somewhere to hide
You're smiling at me
Everything you do
For me.

it's all here
Everything a girl could want
late night talks
goodnight kisses
afternoon movies and snacks
early morning walks

there is only
One love
like mine
True love
between
A girl and her dog.

Gunpowder Hearts II
by Kaitlyn Luckow

Smoke signals
dance on our lips---
A warning
of battles to come
and we're only armed
with our hands
unable to defend
against
our Gunpowder hearts.

"You're In Love With A Memory"
by Rhea Smith

Yeah. I know. You can spare me the lecture.
I really should've known from the get go.
One thing's for certain, she's not the same girl.
I say I know, and yet I really don't.

Why does the heart pine for what isn't real?
Do I blame the heart, the brain, the writer?
Rational thought doesn't dictate the feel.
Yet I find myself ever the fighter.

She Said
by Cassandra Bankson

"You have no idea what you're getting yourself into",
She said.
"You won't be able to handle it",
She said.
"You need to rethink this"
She said.
"You need to protect yourself"
She said.

I love you
She said.

CHAPTER SEVEN
lust

She's In Each Of Us
by Cassandra Bankson

Her skin knows no boundaries
Her body, no form
Lips speak more than words
And her eyes could transform
A calm passerby
On an evening train
To a ravaged casualty
Of pleasure and shame
An addict is born
By a glance or a look
The stroke of soft fingers
Pierce rational like a hook
The way that a novel
Keeps you turning its page
The enigma of "female"
Locks your heart in her cage
Friction and greed
Hot air burns when inhaled
A magnetic smile
That leaves you assailed
Feeding carnal hunger
She wants bodies untrussed
She's beauty, desire,
But I call her Lust.
(she's in each of us)

Connect
by Eileen Ramos

Bare your skin,
beneath the ice,
cold to touch
the warmth sufficed.

Drawn to you,
a fevered stare.
Sweat slow down
through tangled hair.

Sweet, soft, curves,
a bitten lip.
Your eyes' pool,
I want a sip.

Blaze a trail
From neck to thigh.
Wet hot mouth,
a pent-up sigh.

Feel your heat.
Witness release.
Let it rise
and walls decrease.

Seek my burn,
you are the source.
Show me now
How your floe's scorched.

As you melt,
within my grasp,
pull me close.

Hear worlds collapse.

Lonely Lust
by Haley Littlefield

Sometimes I feel so empty inside
I miss his touch
I need him to fill that void
Sensuality and sadness must be sisters
My body can't have one without the other
He is like a rock.
So strong and solid.
I can throw myself on him.
He can bear that weight.
But I have no idea what he's feeling.
Like a fucking rock.

"Boys Like You"
by Cassandra Bankson

All those unsent letters
That "girls like us"
Write to "boys like you"

What we unravel from inside ourselves
We somehow manage to weave into words.

Spinning sentences like a spider
In attempts to make a hammock a home
But it's more an opportunity for relaxation
Versus walls that provide value or protection.

Similar to the home I've learned
Wasn't a home
Just the comfortable hammock
Of your rented heart

And so we spill words
like a glass of water across this page
Only some pages aren't that absorbent
Like you when you listen.

I would imagine
That listening with your eyes
still isn't an option
So curse the cursive

I'll make it a point
To conveniently forget to lick the stamp
The way I'll try conveniently
To forget you

Oh the things "girls like us" would say
to "boys like you".

Thoughts During Sex
by Lily LeFebvre

"Burning Passion".
Sounds like such a cliché.
But every cliché exists for a reason, right?
An ache deep in your chest. Warmth. Fire.
A very need to mesh our bodies into one.

"Getting Down and Dirty".
Isn't it though?
At the time, it feels so right.
But I look back and I see a crime.
That, I'll chalk up to conditioning.
There's nothing wrong with my desire.

"Doing the Deed."
Seriously, are we twelve?
Who says that anymore?
Just shut your mouth and kiss me.

Your fingers might get stuck in my hair.
I might accidentally knee you in the groin.
I was just trying to get on top, I swear.
Oh God, do I smell bad?
Forget it. You smell so good.
Or maybe they're pheromones.

All I know is
I want to drag my nails down your back.
I want to bite into your lip, hard.
Where did this come from, why so violent?

Burning. Dirty. The Deed can hurt.
"Hurts So Good" doesn't even touch it.

CHAPTER EIGHT
etc.

Talk is Talk is Talk is Talk…
by Lily LeFebvre

"Oh, she's a serial monogamist."
Yeah, so that means you should stay away, right?
"She's codependent. Not a realist."
You know that about me after one night?

"She's high-maintenance, she's so not worth it."
Says he who maintains his car more than me.
"Trust me, you'll quickly get tired of her bit."
You're tired of the one who's restrained, you see.

I got tired of biting my tongue around you.
Tired of laughing at jokes that weren't funny.
Tired of agreeing with things that weren't true.
Stormy demeanor? Less 'bright and sunny'.

Maybe I'm better off as a cynic.
Better that than being a chronic dick.

Alyssa Paxson

The Dog and the Butterfly
by Meg Colt

A dog and a butterfly met in a wood
while following a leaf covered path
the butterfly was out for recreation
the dog avoiding a bath

The dog was intrigued by the butterfly
her wings fluttered so fast
The butterfly found him comical
she studied him as he ran past

The butterfly's wings quivered
she was ready for a race
the dog galloped effortlessly
flawlessly keeping pace

The dog overtook his companion
as he rounded the second bend
the butterfly's resolve hardened
determined to beat her new friend

The butterfly saw the obstacle
but regrettably the dog did not
distracted by thoughts and nature
his paw was gashed on a rock

The dog's glimmer faded
his ego had been hurt
he sat down defeated
gazing at the dirt

The butterfly floated over
her wings brilliant and bright
and in a clear gesture of forfeit
landed to his right

So the two sat together
the dog nursed his paw
and there was no winner
just a mutual draw

Alyssa Paxson

Midnight Blooms I
by Kaitlyn Luckow

She draws her future
in rocks,
hoping they won't be
    washed away
by the heart. beat. sea.
As she stands herself
open-armed to the waves.

Alyssa Paxson

Counting
by Cassandra Bankson

How many drafts before naked words are outfitted into poems?
How many strokes before a canvas windows perceptions of life?
How many letters before metaphor spills veracity?
How many keys before decibels evoke emotion?
How many dreams before the mind becomes a mirror?
An artist's work is never completed, only abandoned.

Alyssa Paxson

Hole
by Haley Littlefield

I thought you were my destiny
I loved you even though I never saw you
I held you even though we never met

But love does not come without a cost
It is pain and grief
It is loss and sorrow

When you were taken, it left a hole inside of me
It created an emptiness I could have never imagined
You were an ending I didn't think I could live through

I have felt true meaninglessness
Anxiety and depression tried desperately to fill the hole
But they failed and left me raw and open

All I hoped for was some solace
Something to fill that hole you left
Something to plug the vacuum my body created without me

And then she came
This beautiful gift
A flicker of life ready to change me forever

I was flooded with emotions
Joy, relief, fear, and disbelief
Is this really happening, is it finally over

Still somehow the hole remained
How can I truly love her when I lost you
How can I love you without denying her

Why is guilt the price I pay for love
I am so alone though I'm living for two
Why must I say goodbye to one joy to greet another

If you had stayed, she wouldn't have come
To have her, I had to lose you
I can't have one without the loss of the other

I feel her tiny flutters
And I feel my love growing
But still the hole remains

SENSITIVE & STRONG AS HELL

Natalie Meagan

Midnight Blooms II
by Kaitlyn Luckow

I sleep with birds
who echo in my ribs
the melody of
reaching branches
and moonlight blooms,
of notes
to let my cage know
it has always been
        Free.

why don't you cry about it

Second Thoughts
by Rebecca Foley

I don't care about
collecting rocks or painting
a smile on my face
if I disappeared
Would you even care

Trying Heroin and
Cocaine looking for
the stairway to
Nowhere if I found it
Would you even care

Thoughts
All of them
banging around
too many
Please

Would you even care
if I opened up
to you did you even
Notice the scars on
my heart on my wrists

Would you even care
if all I left was
One word a cry
for help one word
Good-Bye.

Natalie Meagan

The Irony That Day
by Rhea Smith

Now they say all is fair in love and war
But isn't it telling to compare them?
I have no desire to seek anymore
And to seek love and sex – what an omen!
What we call love is brittle, and fickle,
And I want nothing to do with either.
Your heart might flutter, your chest might tickle
They're all just chemical, when you see her.
Never thought I'd see casualties in love
I'd heard the stories but never seen it
I beg not to fall, whoever's above
"In love" no more, and I truly mean it.

About the Collective

Cassandra Bankson - Author
It is not unusual to find Cassandra Bankson with her nose in a book. This time, however, she has stuck her tongue into one. Cassandra started writing poetry as a form of therapy, in attempts to express herself, in a way that only writing can heal. She didn't start taking her short stories and poems seriously until she realized penning her experiences could also help others heal. Her writing has evolved to cover various topics: from admiring the intention that a small seed has to sprout into a lace-limbed tree, to exploring the dark cryptic corners of our minds that we use to keep our dusty secrets in, to a word we call "love". Outside of papers and pens, she enjoys hiking, traveling, playing piano, spontaneous adventures with friends, and cuddling with her six cats. Although acne got the best of her skin and self esteem for a large portion of the past 15 years, Cassandra found confidence in a stick of concealer that enabled her to become an international runway model, a far stretch from the bullied teenage runaway she was just a few years prior. For the past seven years, she has pioneered the online space of beauty, challenging what it is, how we perceive it, how we define it, and how we express it. She has also worked on various projects, including clothing and jewelry lines, an app, a nonprofit organization, and most recently a digital magazine called "Inspire". She continues to create YouTube videos containing make up tricks, self development tools, and inspiration. A student at Stanford University, she is working towards an undeclared degree in pre-medicine in hopes of changing the way doctors treat our bodies, skin, and acne - and the emotions that come with it. Cassandra is a firm believer that challenges are growth opportunities in disguise, and she hopes that by sharing her experiences, others can learn and grow from these same lessons as well to live beautifully, both inside and out.

Caz Brett - Author
Caz has always been surprised that the men in white coats did not take her away when she wrote a short poem about dead pigs when she was five. She is a feminist and all-round creative person from London, and also writes short stories and personal pieces, often covering subjects like depression and anxiety. She enjoys avoiding the news, imagining her life if she were married to Tina Fey, and the feeling of writing on a banana in biro.

Meg Colt - Author
Meg began writing short stories and poetry at the age of eight. She was always enthralled with literature, and it was no surprise to anyone when she graduated college with a Bachelor of Arts in English. Besides guest blogging on other platforms, Meg also authors her own blog, Irrevocably in Reverie. It is there

that she tackles body positive activism, eating disorder recovery, and mental health awareness. Writing was a form of therapy for her as a child, and that hasn't changed in the slightest now that she is in her mid-twenties. Meg also hopes to eventually get a Master's degree in Library Science, so she can actualize her dream of becoming a librarian. When she isn't writing, Meg can usually be found chasing her three children or drinking iced coffee.

Lucy Ellerton - Author
Lucy has been reading and writing on and off for years, so much so that she decided to do an Arts degree. To pass on her love for literature and the dramatic arts, she made sure to get an Education degree at the same time. Currently after a break of a year to fully realize her goals, she wants to work on reading, writing, exploring, and passing on her love for all those things to high school students.

Rebecca Foley - Author
Rebecca has been writing since she was eight years old. One of the first pieces she can remember writing was a series of short mysteries about three detectives named "Me, Myself, and I". Though she has moved past writing about "Me, Myself, and I", she still looks back on those stories to remind her of how far she has come and where her love for writing began. Now at the age of 21, she is working towards a Children's Literature Bachelor's degree from Eastern Michigan University. After graduating, she hopes to work in a library, while continuing to write. She is scared but eager to share her work with the world for the first time. When she is not writing, she can be found surrounded by others' stories, whether it be through books, movies, or TV shows. She has always been fascinated by the story and hopes to one day have others fascinated and inspired by hers. Her writing style consists of mostly fiction in the prose form, but she has branched out into poetry. She has a wonderful family – a mom, dad, older brother and loving dog – who support her in all that she wants to accomplish.

Lily LeFebvre - Author
Lily began writing short stories at the young age of seven, but this publication marks the first that has reached a wider audience than a small writer's forum. It's no secret that her father is a literature and linguistics professor at a university – one that she'd prefer not to name – and thus has passed on that love for language. Around thirteen, she fell in love with the Shakespearean and Petrarchan sonnet, and for years wrote with the same strict formatting in all of her works. Now at eighteen, she's learning to expand and let go of that strictness with her writing, allowing for more free verse poetry. She attends a fairly well known boarding school in California as a senior, and is an active member of the GSA and school writer's forum. When she's not writing or studying for her classes, Lily enjoys running track and sketching portraits - however bad they may be - of her closest friends. Her next big tasks are to

graduate and travel around Europe (particularly England, France, and Italy) before attending NYU.

Chelsea Lewis - Artist
Chelsea "Rue" Lewis is an artistic spirit that can only be sighted on rare occasions, crawling out from the depths of dreams once every few years to spit out physical manifestations of her creativity in the form of colored pencil illustrations and the written word. Currently this mythical creature is a patron of humanity's young, caring for them and enjoying the refreshing authenticity, brutal honesty, and creativity that comes from fledgling minds. Rue has visions of one day being invoked to illustrate, publish volumes of poetry, write and illustrate children's books, and generally shake up the greeting card industry (watch out, Hallmark). If you'd like to study this apparition more, Rue and her work can best be found on Instagram at @chelsea.lew and @rueable.

Caroline Linford - Artist
Kittypinkstars… a shooting star that fell to the sea... waiting for her spaceship, one day she'll go home, but until then... cover the world in her rainbow and sprinkle a little sunshine daily!

Haley Littlefield - Author
Haley has always loved the written word. Her earliest work that she can recall was a short story about giant birds taking over the world. She wrote this at the age of eleven, shortly after being pecked on the head by what she is sure was, in fact, a giant bird. In recent years, her writing has been very personal, mostly journaling as a means of self-care. She graduated from the University of Texas at Dallas with a B.A. in Literary Studies in 2013. She spent her college career focused mostly on attempting to not overuse commas. During college and after graduation, she worked at a local library caressing the precious books (not in her job description, it's fine) for six years until she left her position to pursue her greatest adventure yet, herself. The last year has been an amazing journey. As scary as it is to share her writing with the world, it feels truly liberating. Haley can often be found drinking a warm beverage from one of her many adorable mugs, usually with a book (or a dog) nearby. She is currently expecting her first child with her husband, Robert. They live in Rowlett, Texas with their dogs, Waffles and Robin, and their fish, Remus, Aloysius, Hyde, and Iago. Commas and giant birds remain her biggest enemies.

Kaitlyn Luckow – Author, Editor
Kaitlyn is a high school English teacher by day and co-founder of The Crybaby Club by night. She's adored writing her whole life and has loved exploring different genres. Along with writing, her passions include photography, reading, petting stranger's dogs and eating an infinite amount of doughnuts. In

her poetry, she likes to explore different ideas regarding beauty and the universal human experience.

Hannah Maine - Author
Hannah has always found comfort in the written word, whether that be getting lost inside fictional stories or expressing her feelings in fervish journal entries. She attended the University of Michigan to pursue a Bachelor of Arts in English and a minor in writing. It was there that she grew as a writer and found a passion for nonfiction writing. Hannah now uses her passion for writing to advocate for mental health awareness at her blog Totally Mental and its corresponding Instagram @totally.mental. She has always been attracted to the way readers are able to feel new emotions and experiences through the written word, and she hopes to give and receive new experiences in this publication.

Natalie Meagan - Artist
Natalie Meagan is an artist, occasional writer and founder of The Crybaby Club. She lives in Memphis, Tennessee with her two sons, Jack and Samson, and their dog, Cheese. She has been emotional and artistic for seemingly her entire life, and has since learned to combine those characteristics and use them to help spread message of female empowerment and crybaby pride to sensitive souls and empaths all over the world. It is her dream to meet and hug as many crybabies as she can in her lifetime, lead by example in supporting and lifting all women, and continue making a difference with her art.

Kayley Mills - Artist
Kayley Mills is 27 and lives in Newcastle, UK. She's a part time illustrator and an Etsy store owner (https://www.etsy.com/uk/shop/KayleyDraws). She has always loved drawing since she was a kid; she used to come home from school and it would be the first thing she wanted to do. She used to draw all sorts, from Mr. Men, people, to anything Disney related (some things never change)! Art has always been her biggest passion. Her other hobbies include going to the theatre (she's a massive musical nerd), pole fitness, and travelling! When she's not drawing, she also loves going on adventures on the weekend with her other half and pup!

Alyssa Paxson - Author, Artist
Alyssa has kept a journal off and on for longer than she can remember. (She once found a journal so old it had "the" spelled "tha" because it was sounded out). She attended an arts high school where, in addition to playing flute in orchestra, she participated in a number of small ensembles, including chamber groups, jazz band (on tenor sax), and pit orchestra for "Pirates of Penzance" and "Meet Me In St. Louis". Her focus switched to studio art at Florida Southern College, where she earned a BFA in oil painting and went on to work as the school's gallery director and Fine Arts division secretary. At 32, Alyssa now

works from home on her Etsy shop, Burrow & Bloom, while caring for and homeschooling her son, Fox. She is grateful for the support of her husband, friends, and family.

Eileen Ramos - Author, Editor
Eileen is a queer Filipina-American writer with bipolar disorder and a history of psychoses. As a mental health advocate, she is the head event and donation space coordinator for The Asian American Literary Review's "Open in Emergency: A Special Issue on Asian American Mental Health". Her very first monologue was published within the *In Full Color* anthology which contains poetry and monologues by women of color. She will perform on the *In Full Color* stage with her monologue "Psychotic Break" and while she's extremely anxious, it feels utterly right. Other things she wants to do that terrify her with how much desire and hold they have over her include: publish an experimental, interactive book with a joint comic book; leave guerrilla art across the U.S.A and all over the world; and have a real life meet-cute where she flirts first with someone at a bookstore and buys them the book they're carrying as well as a favorite she knows they'll love. Past and forthcoming publications include the zines *White Man's Burden*, *Ano Ba*, and *Hoax*. You can find her on Instagram and Twitter as @eintervital.

Kimberley Robinson - Artist
Kimberley Robinson is the founder of the British brand Keep Real - a clothing and goods business aiming to grow and inspire well-being, especially in young people. She loves to get creative and is super passionate about raising awareness in mental health. Her many loves include Patti Smith, saying the word 'wizard' and weeping through memes about cute dogs on the internet.

Rhea Smith - Author, Head Editor
At the age of 23, Rhea has nearly 12 years of writing under her belt. Rather than running around outside as a child, she stayed inside and perfected her spelling to prepare for tests she was determined to ace. Granted, this was under the watchful scrutiny of her mother, but to this day she is grateful for the strict academic mindset. (Since then, her spelling has slipped little-by-little, but hey, that's what autocorrect is for!) She went to UC-Davis to study Biological Sciences, with an emphasis on Medical Microbiology, but never gave up writing as a hobby. She briefly wrote for Spoon.com before graduating university, and has written pieces for several publications released by her previous schools. While in university, she found her love for dogs when she began fostering for the YOLO County SPCA - and while she doesn't currently own a dog, she can't wait until she has the stability to take care of her own. When she's not writing, Rhea can be found experimenting with her guitar, singing at the top of her lungs, or practicing self-care in the form of face masks

and good books. After publication, her next big goal is to get into dental school and pursue periodontics.

Louisa Tracey - Author
Louisa Tracey is 30 years old and hails from Glasgow, Scotland. Born in a nearby smaller town, she moved to the big smoke to study Professional Cookery. After graduating in the summer of 2016, she now works full time as a chef. Food is her life in many ways. She also loves animals, traveling and collecting pop culture merch and cute art. A feminist and a socialist, she is always finding a new cause to fight for. Writing has been a life long hobby of Louisa's, both for fun and catharsis. Louisa's spare time is also filled with escaping to other worlds and hanging out with fictional characters through books, TV, films and games. She hopes to become a head chef and dreams big of owning a food business one day.

www.ingramcontent.com/pod-product-compliance
Lightning Source LLC
Chambersburg PA
CBHW022106160426
43198CB00008B/373